GW01044434

Suzuki®Violin School

VIOLIN PART
VOLUME 9

CONTENTS

Concerto in A Major

コンチェルト

イ長調

Wolfgang Amadeus Mozart
Joachim - Suzuki

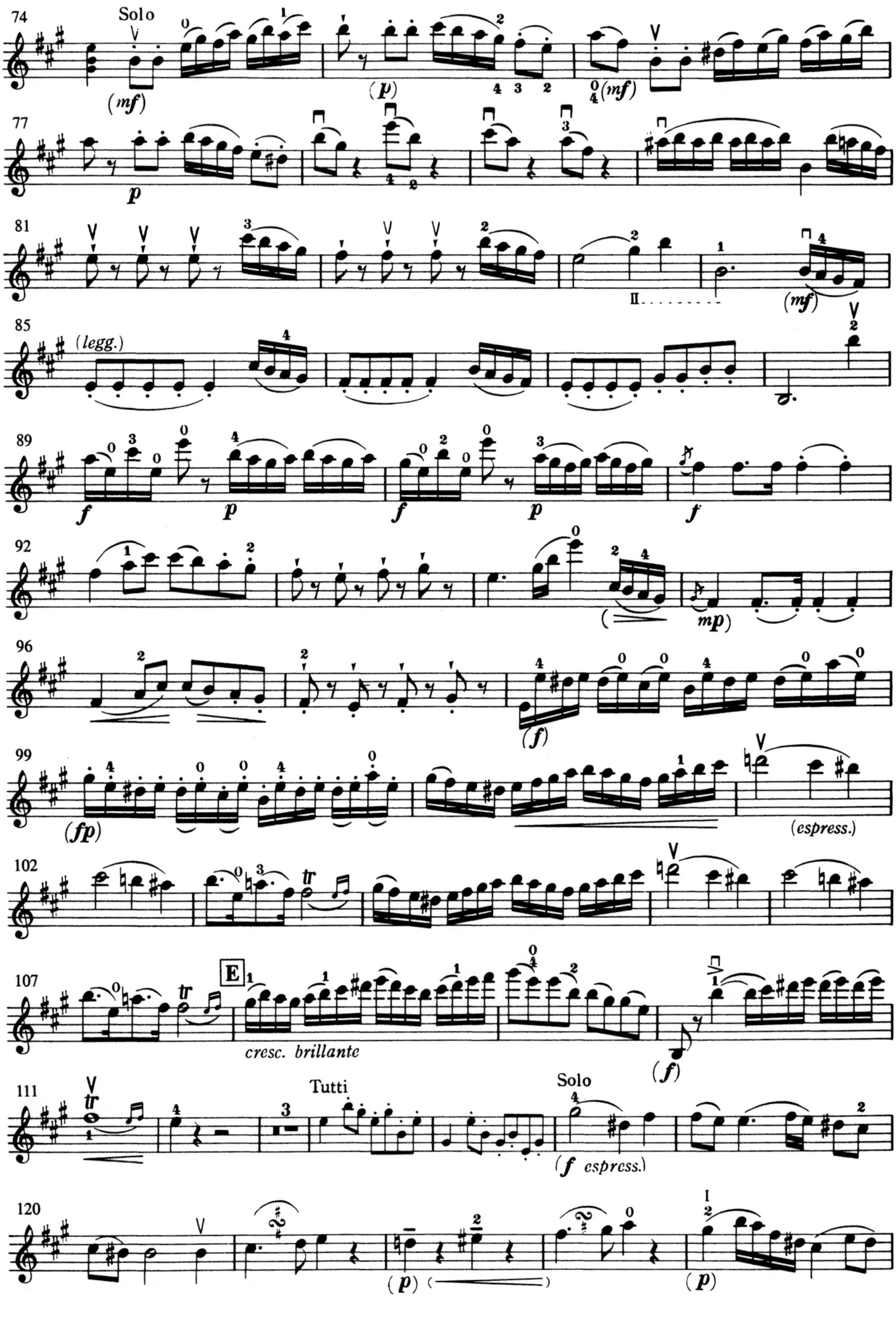
Solo
(legg.)
(espress.)
cresc. brillante
Tutti
Solo
(f espress.)

8

Rondo
Tempo di Minuetto (♩ = 112-126)

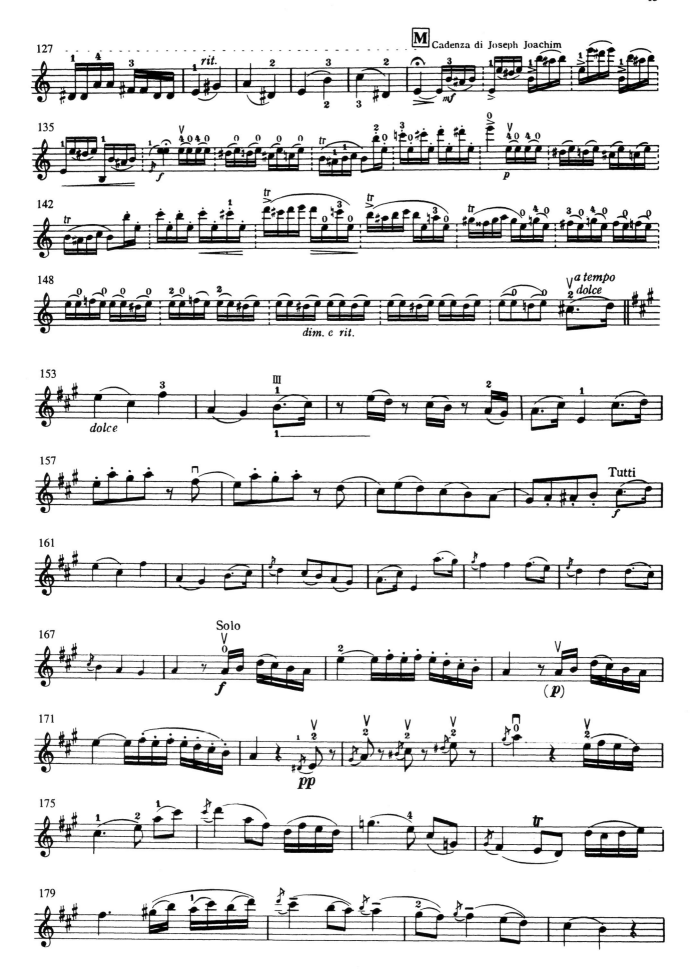

The First Movement
第一楽章

Point of Practice

Many pupils, when they have learned to play, are apt to become self-satisfied and give up further practice. But if they ever want to cultivate superior ability, they still need to continue their daily practice, always trying to improve their performance, even if they already can play 'correctly'. One should never forget that one's ability will be fostered in proportion to the amount of one's diligent and steady practice.

学習の仕方

どうにか弾けるようになると、多くの人は安心して訓練をやめてしまいがちです。高い能力を得た人はまちがいなく弾けるようになってからも、さらによりよくなるために毎日繰り返しているのです。
本当の能力というものは、どれほどそれを繰り返したかによって育っていくものなのです。

Fundamental Exercise 基本練習

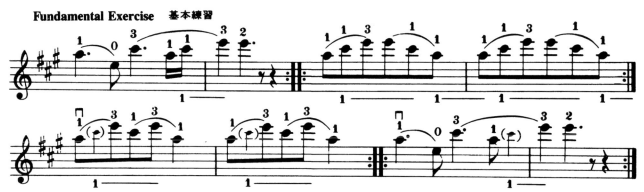

Practise each exercise over and over, and do not proceed to the next section before you are sure of playing this one well. Each succeeding repetition should be practised in this way.
Note: play slowly and accurately.

リピートのあるところを納得のいくまで繰り返し、つづいて次の小節へ弾きつづけていくやり方をしてください。
以下全部このやり方で行ない、毎日繰り返す。
注意：ゆっくりと、正しく弾ける速さで。

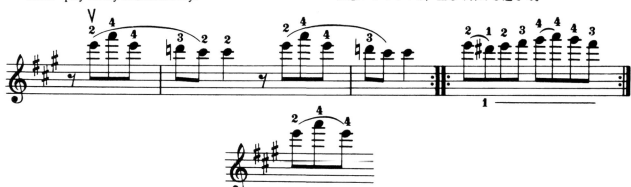

In this placing of fingers, the descending movement of the fourth finger (4-4) is likely to become unsteady if it is done by moving the fourth finger independently. In order to give it stability, learn to change position with the first finger following together with the fourth.

この押え方は、単に4—4だけで下ると不安定です。そのために1の指をつけたままでポジションの移動を訓練し安定感をつくります。

4の指を押えたとき、2をはなして1・4の形にし、そして1・4のままで下っていきます。

When you have placed the fourth finger, raise the second finger to form the shape 1·4, and continue to descend with this shape unchanged.

Note: Where the indication tr. is given, first practise without the ornament, and then practise as designated.

注意：トリル記号のあるものは、はじめトリルをつけないで、まず上記のように原形を練習して、その後に装飾をつけること。

Note: Make sure that the two fingers are prepared in place before you start to play the trill.

このとき1の指をあらかじめ押えておくこと。

To play this figure, the first finger should be placed beforehand.

トリルを弾く前に3の指を迅速に押える練習をすること。このとき前以って1の指が押えてあることは最も効果的である。

Before actually playing the trill, go through the exercise for rapid placing of the third finger. This figure can be executed most effectively if the first finger is placed in advance.

注意：トリルは事前に2つの指の準備完了を行なうこと。

前列と同じように2のときに1の指をつけることと、トリルのための3の指を速く準備する訓練が必要です。

In playing this figure, you again need to place the first and second fingers together and rapidly get the third finger prepared for the trill.

Point of Practice

学習の仕方

E弦からA弦へ移るときの左手の訓練で、A弦→D弦、D弦→G弦の場合も同じです。

Train the left hand for changing strings from E to A. Also practise change of strings from A to D, and from D to G.

For detailed explanation, the position of the right hand to play should be slightly raised toward the position of double stopping on the E and the A strings. Then change strings by slightly raising the right hand fingers (which hold the bow) when the third finger is moved to the A string. The wrist should not be raised.

くわしく説明すると、 のときに右手の位置がE弦、A弦の重音を弾く位置へかすかにあげられ、3の指でA弦に移るときに右手指（弓をもつ指）がわずかに上へあがることによって移弦をする。手首が上へあがるのはいけない。

同じようにそれぞれの移弦の練習をゆっくりと練習する。

In the same way practice changing strings carefully on each pair of strings.

(A) (D) (G)

Preparation of the First Finger

1の指の準備

The following instruction for practice will serve further to improve you in executing downward changes of position.

While the second finger in third position is playing this passage, keep the first finger attached to the second finger, and the moment you place the fourth finger, lift the second finger alone, leaving the first finger where it is. In other words, the movement which starts with the fourth finger should proceed downward led by the first finger, thus changing to the first position through shifting from the first to the second finger. If the second finger of the third position were given the initiative in such change of position, (that is, the fourth, the third and the second fingers were placed separately one after another centering around the second finger), the pitches would easily become faulty because you will then have to place the first finger anew, which in turn must be immediately shifted to the second finger of the first position.

This should always be kept in mind as it is applicable to many cases appearing later.

下向へのポジション移動の熟練のために、練習の仕方を参考に記しておきましょう。

譜のように、サード・ポジションの2の指を弾いているときに2の指に1の指C♯をつけておき、4の指を弾くと同時に1の指だけを残して2の指を離す。すなわち4の指からの進行を、1の指を基本として下行して、1から2の指（ファースト・ポジション）へ移す練習をする。サード・ポジションで2の指を基本にして4・3・2と弾いていくと、1の指を新たに押えなければならず、押えるとすぐにまたファースト・ポジションの2の指へ変っていくことになり、不安定になるからです。

このことは今後いろいろな場合に応用ができます。

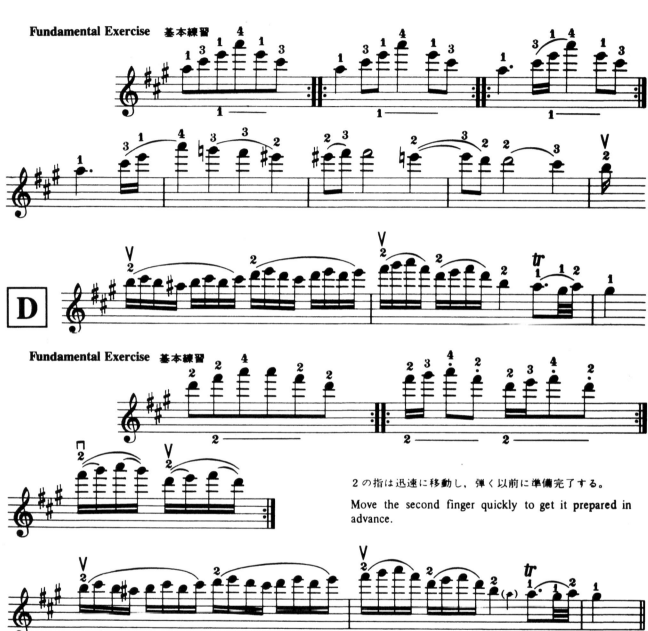

2の指は迅速に移動し，弾く以前に準備完了する。

Move the second finger quickly to get it prepared in advance.

While playing the second finger, be sure to attach the first finger to it.

2の指を弾いている間に1の指をつける練習をする。

4の指を正確に押える練習。このときの2の指を押えたとき4の指も押えてみる。小指が高いところに位置する習慣を少しでも正していく。

Place the fourth finger accurately.
When you place the second finger to play this note, also put the fourth finger down by way of trial just to avoid forming the bad habit of letting it play sharp.

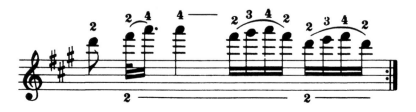

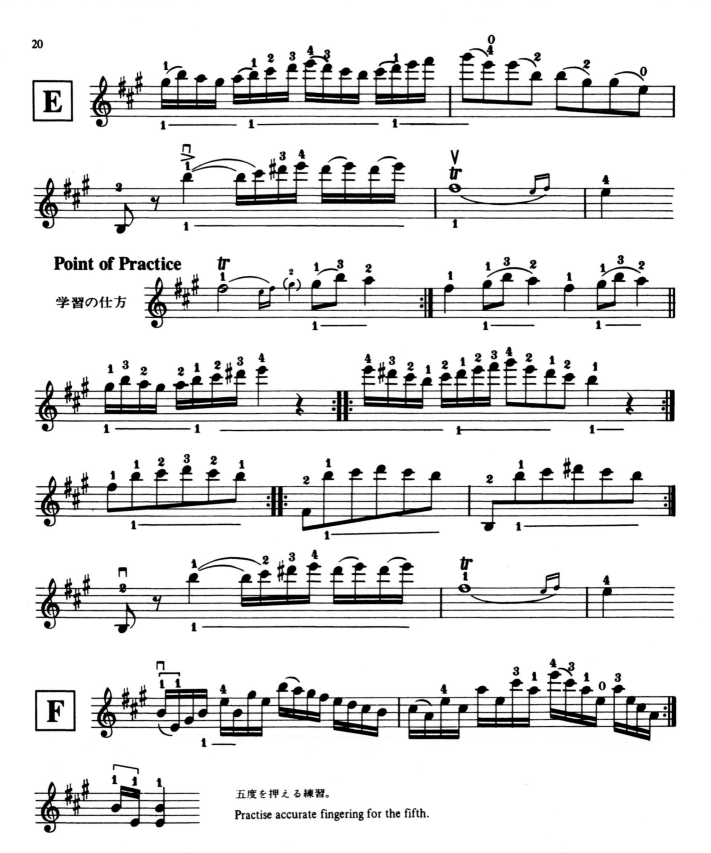

Point of Practice

学習の仕方

Practise accurate fingering for the fifth.

五度を押える練習。

Point of Practice　　学習の仕方

Exercise of Changing Strings, Which Corresponds with B

B と同じ移動の訓練

Do not strain the right wrist. This is especially important for those who are liable to pull back their elbow. You must not allow the bow to bounce and must play legato. In practising change of strings, it is essential to play slowly and repeatedly.

右手首をかたくならないようにし、とくに右のひじがうしろへひき気味の人は注意すること。また弓をはずませないでレガートで弾きます。とくに移弦の練習は、ゆっくりと繰り返し行なうことがたいせつです。

Point of Practice　　学習の仕方

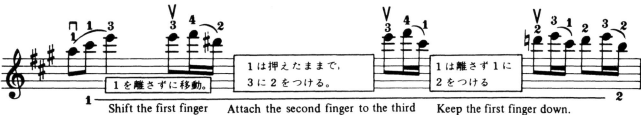

1を離さずに移動。

Shift the first finger without raising it.

1は押えたままで、3に2をつける。

Attach the second finger to the third finger, keeping the first finger placed on the string.

1は離さず1に2をつける

Keep the first finger down.

3に2をつける。

Attach the second finger to the third finger.

1に2をつける。

Attach the second finger to the first finger.

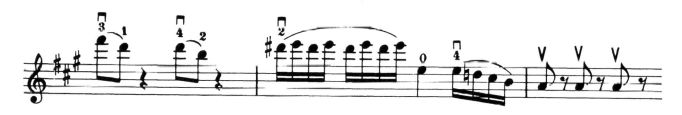

Point of Practice　　学習の仕方

Practise the whole passage every day, repeating the fundamental figures until you can play them with confidence.

基本的な練習を納得のいくまで繰り返しながら、毎日通してひく。

弓をA弦の位置に安定させてから次をひく。
(Put the bow firmly on the A string before proceeding to the next notes.)

Join the second finger to the third finger.

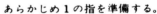

Prepare the first finger beforehand.

あらかじめ1の指を準備する。

While playing the open E string, put the first finger at its proper place on the A string, and prepare it in advance so that the 1⌒4 fingering may be fixed accurately. Always try to obtain exact pitches, aiming at still more improved and refined performance.

音程を正しくとり，よりいっそう洗練された演奏になるよう心がける。
E弦の開放を弾いている間に1の指をA弦に正しく位置し，⌒14の指使いが正確に押えられるように，あらかじめ準備する。

Practice should always be done thoughtfully and with the greatest possible care.

訓練は常に細心の注意と合理の上に行なわれなければならない。

Point of Practice 　　学習の仕方

Practise each fundamental exercise twenty times every day, and as you get skilful, gradually increase the speed.

それぞれの基本練習は毎日20回くらい繰り返して弾き、熟練するにしたがって速度を速くする。

This is how I usually study a piece of music myself. Daily repetition will make it seem easier and easier, and that means genuine ability is being developed. If you continue to practise every day even after you have learned to play fairly well, you will certainly gain substantial proficiency, which then will grow to be superior capability applicable to any piece of music.

私が学習するときはいつもこのようにやっています。毎日繰り返してやっている間にだんだんやさしく感じられてくるようになり、それが実力の育った証拠です。一応演奏できていてもなお毎日繰り返している間に、本当の能力が高められ、他の曲の場合においても応用できる、すぐれた能力へ育っていくわけです。

24

Point of Practice　学習の仕方

While Joachim gave the above fingering to this passage, the second position, as shown below, was indicated by Karl Klingler, my old teacher. The merit of the latter might be that there is no positional unsteadiness in the first and the second beats of the third measure.

上の譜の指使いはヨアヒムのものであるが、私の師事したカール・クリンクラーはセカンド・ポジションを示したので、参考に記しておく。3小節目の1，2拍のポジションの不安定感がないのが特長といえるであろう。

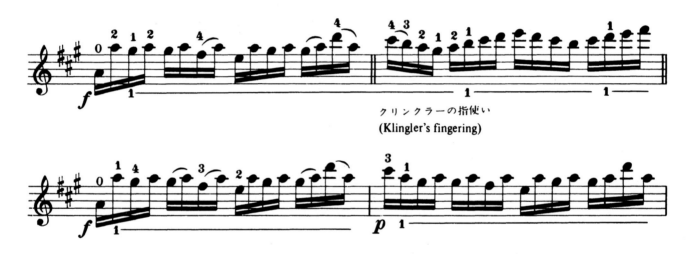

クリンクラーの指使い
(Klingler's fingering)

Play the second measure *p*, and study how to make obvious the contrast between *f* and *p*
Play accurately in pitch.

2小節目の最初の一音を *p* でひく練習を行ない、*f* と *p* のはっきりした差をつくる訓練を行なう。
音程を正しくすること。

Play slowly at first with accurate intonation, and then gradually increase speed.

おそくても正しい音程で弾きながら、しだいに速度をあげる。

Point of Practice　学習の仕方

Fundamental Exercise　基本練習

音程を正確に。
Accurate intonation

ゆっくり正確に。
Slowly and accurately

この音程が正しくとれるように
訓練する。

Practise these intervals with accurate intonation.

To secure correct pitch, place the first finger accurately and then play the fourth, the third, the second and the first fingers in this order.

音程を正しくとるために1の指を正確に押えて4321と練習する。

Cadenza
カ デ ン ツ

Point of Practice　学習の仕方

Play slowly and accurately, making contrast between *f*
and *p*

ゆっくり正確にひき，*f* と *p* の差の練習を行なう。

1の指を離さない。
Do not raise the first finger.

cresc.

In order to obtain the exact pitch, the fourth finger
should be played while the first finger is kept on the string.
Learn to place the fourth finger almost in advance.

音程を正しくとるために，1を押えたまま4を弾く練習。
4の指を先に押えるくらいに練習すること。

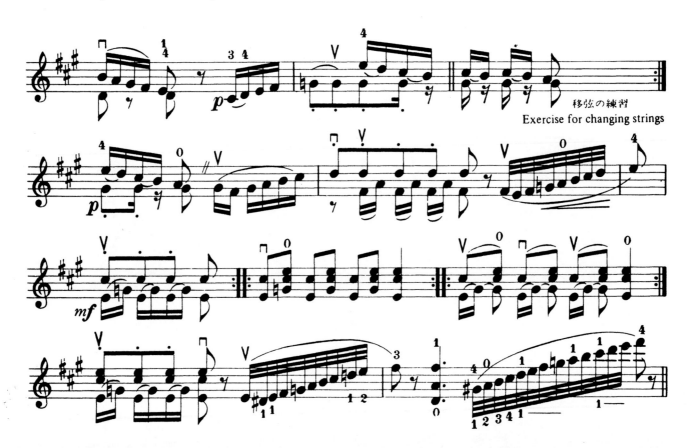

移弦の練習
Exercise for changing strings

ゆっくり音程の練習。
Play slowly with accurate pitch.

2に1の指をつける。
Keep the first finger close
to the second finger.

2/3で押える音を正確にすること。
The pitches of 2/3 should be
accurate.

洗練された音を出す練習。
Try to produce refined tone.

Count exactly, and play the slur with moderate bow.

拍子を正しくとり、スラーで弾くときの弓は余裕をもっ
て弾く。

トリルの基本練習——トリルを弾くまえに2，3の指を
迅速に押える。
Fundamental Trill Exercise: Place the second and the
third fingers rapidly before playing the trill.

音程の練習
Exercise for
Exact Intervals

Learn to place fingers at the correct interval, and play slowly at first without slurring. After you have learned to play the slur, there shouldn't be the least unevenness.

最初にスラー無しでゆっくり練習し、指と音程の練習をする。拍子に乱れがあってはいけません。

dolce

cresc.

largamente

音程訓練
Exercise for
Correct Intervals

1，2の指をつける。
Keep the first and second fingers close together.

cresc. e stringendo

1の指を離さない。
Do not lift
the first finger.

sf のアコードの練習
Practise the sf chord.

移弦の鮮明さを出す。
Change strings as clearly as possible.

3つに分れている弓の位置を正確に。
Learn the exact positions of these three stages in bowing.

4，3，2の指をつける。
The fourth, the third
and the second fingers
are close together.

✗の音が正しいか確認する
Make sure that the tone
marked with ✗ is accurate
in pitch.

と同じ

2の指に3，4をつ
ける音程練習。

Keep the third finger close to the second finger, and the
fourth finger close to the third finger for an accurate interval.

Practise the fundamental exercises every day, especially
concentrating on such passages as you find difficult.
First try to play accurately even in the slowest tempo
according to your own ability at the moment, and then
gradually accelerate till you get to the required speed.

基本的な訓練を毎日繰り返し，とくにむずかしいと感ず
るところを重点的に行なう。速度は自分の能力に応じて，
はじめはなるべくゆっくり正確に弾き，しだいに速度を
あげ，必要な速さにまで達する。

The Second Movement
Adagio
第二楽章　　ア ダ ー ジョ

Point of Practice　　　学習の仕方

2，3の指の準備
Prepare the second
and the third fingers
properly.

Point of Practice　　　学習の仕方

ヨアヒムの指使いです。3－3の移り方
を美しくうたうように練習する。
This is Joachim's fingering. Try to make
the 3-3 shift sing beautifully.

2の指に1の指をつける練習。
（2の指の位置を先に）
Keep the first finger close to
the second finger.
(Place the second finger in advance,)

espress.

lusingando

D♯を弾くときには，E弦とA弦のEの
正確な音を確かめてから。

2の指を3の指につける。

Before playing D♯ make sure that the E's on the E string
and the A string are a perfect unison.

Keep the second finger close to the third
finger.

D

Point of Practice　　学習の仕方

Point of Practice 学習の仕方

音程を正しくとる。2の指に1の指をつける。
Play with accurate pitch. Keep the first finger close to the second finger.

2の指に1の指をつける。
Keep the first finger close to the second finger.

3の指を押えたときに1の指を押える練習をする。
When you place the third finger, be sure to keep the first finger down.

上の指をつけて上下するときの音程の正しさを得る練習。
Learn to obtain accurate pitches in changing position with the first finger down.

Point of Practice　学習の仕方

Fundamental Exercise　基本練習

Cadenza
カデンツ
Point of Practice　　学習の仕方

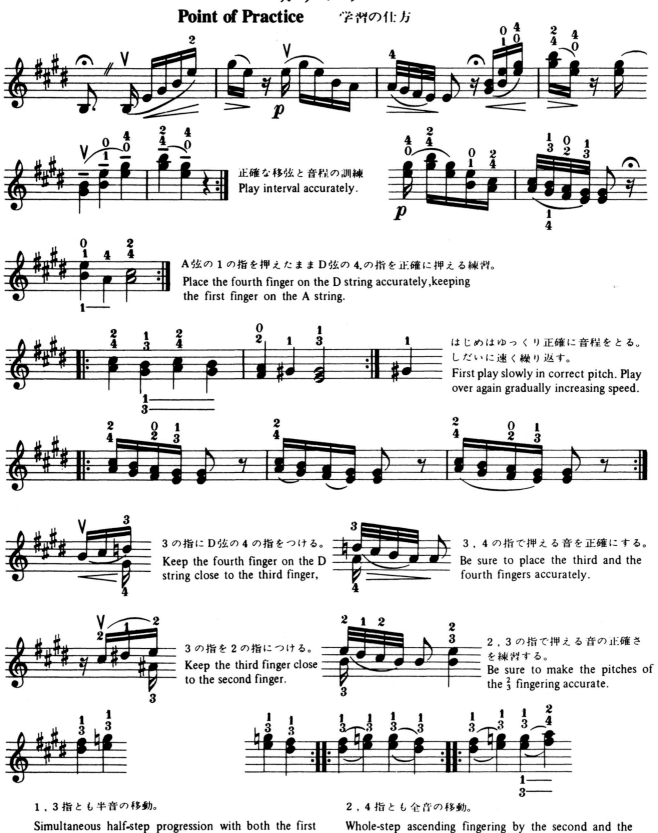

正確な移弦と音程の訓練
Play interval accurately.

A弦の1の指を押えたままD弦の4.の指を正確に押える練習。
Place the fourth finger on the D string accurately, keeping the first finger on the A string.

はじめはゆっくり正確に音程をとる。
しだいに速く繰り返す。
First play slowly in correct pitch. Play over again gradually increasing speed.

3の指にD弦の4の指をつける。
Keep the fourth finger on the D string close to the third finger,

3，4の指で押える音を正確にする。
Be sure to place the third and the fourth fingers accurately.

3の指を2の指につける。
Keep the third finger close to the second finger.

2，3の指で押える音の正確さを練習する。
Be sure to make the pitches of the $\frac{2}{3}$ fingering accurate.

1，3指とも半音の移動。
Simultaneous half-step progression with both the first and the third fingers.

2，4指とも全音の移動。
Whole-step ascending fingering by the second and the fourth fingers.

3の指が低くなりやすいので注意。
Be careful not to let the third finger play flat.

Make sure that the E tone on the A string and that of the open E string are exactly in the same pitch. Keep the second finger close to the first finger, and the fourth finger to the third finger.

A弦のEの音がE弦と同じであるように確かめる。
1の指に2の指を、3の指に4の指をつける練習。

Keep the $\frac{2}{4}$ fingers close to the $\frac{1}{3}$ fingers for correct intervals.
Practise without raising the first and the third fingers.

$\frac{1}{3}$ の指に $\frac{2}{4}$ の指をつけ、音程を正しくとる。1と3の指を押えたままで行なう。

重音を正しく美しく弾くこと。
Try to play the double stops accurately and beautifully.

The above fingering is Joachim's indication. Also practise the alternative fingering given below. It will serve as a good exercise for playing without letting the fingers slide.

以上はヨアヒムの指使いです。終りの部分のもう1つの指づかいを示して置くので、この方も練習するように。指をずらせることなく弾く指づかいです。

3の指をDの1の指につける。
Keep the third finger close to the first finger on the D string.

Keep the three fingers close together, with the first and the second fingers down.
Play the F♯ note on the D string accurately with the third finger.

3本の指をつける。1、2の指を押えたまま。
D弦の3の指によるファ♯の音を正確に。

B

C

練習A，B，Cを順に仕上げていくこと。

音程を確かめて，音程を正しく。
Be careful to make each interval exact.

Fundamental Exercise　基本練習

A……E

Practice this exercise with accurate time and pitch. Play slowly at first according to your ability, and gradually add speed. Unreasonable acceleration will cause unevenness.

この練習では，拍子を正しく，音程を確実に練習します。速度は自分の能力に応じて，はじめはゆっくりひき，だんだん速く練習する。無理をすると乱れのもとになります。

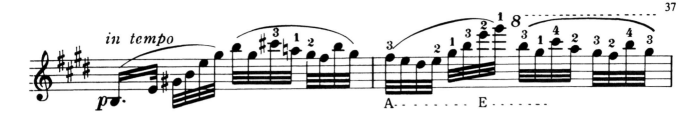

Fundamental Exercise 基本練習

小さいスラーを1つずつ弓を止めて練習。

For exercise, divide the legato slur into pairs of notes and play each small slur with interrupted bow.

Practise very carefully, counting the four beats strictly, until you can play the double-note trill perfectly. Diligent daily practice will surely enable you to play it well.

拍子を4つ正しくとって重音トリルができるまでていねいに練習する。毎日繰り返している人は必ずできるようになります。

拍子を4つとりながら行なうトリルの練習。

Practise these trills, counting four beats accurately.

The Third Movement
Rondo

第三楽章　　ロンド

A

Point of Practice　　　学習の仕方

Fundamental Exercise　基本練習

Do not lift the first finger. Move the first finger accurately to the fifth position.

1の指を離さない。第5ポジションへの1の指の正確な移動を練習する。

注意：最後の音が大きくならないように。

Note: Be careful not to let the last note sound too loud.

B

Point of Practice　　　学習の仕方

Fundamental Exercise　基本練習

2の指に1をつける。　　弓の元の方で。

Keep the first finger close to the second finger.　　Use the lower third of the bow.

正確なセカンド・ポジションをとるように。
Fix the second position exactly.

この音の正しい音程を確かめる。
Make sure that the pitch is correct.

Fundamental Exercise 基本練習

C

(grazioso)

Point of Practice

Direct your attention to grazioso performance in practising this passage, and aim at beautiful expression.

Consider for yourself whether the figure

should be played like ⤜⤛ or otherwise, after actually listening to various excellent performances

The above fingering is Klingler's indication, and the following is Joachim's. Either fingering will result in fine bowing, depending on how it is executed.

学習の仕方

grazioso（優美に）を学習の目標とし、美しい表現を練習する。

この音形を ⤜⤛ のように弾くか、どのように演奏すべきかについては、いろいろ名演奏を聞き、自分でも考えてみてください。

上に記した弓使いは、クリンクラーの示したものであり、下に記したのはヨアヒムのものです。弾き方によってはそのいずれもよい弓使いであると思う。

弓の中央から弾きはじめて ♪ を速い弓の動きで表現する練習。grazioso を忘れないように。

Start playing in the middle of the bow, and try to execute the ornament ♪ with a swift motion. Keep in mind the indication grazioso.

Point of Practice

学習の仕方

While this passage is not necessarily as difficult to play as it looks, there are very few pupils who play it beautifully and perfectly. The most important point in practice is to have sufficient drill on such passages if you are to attain the finest possible performance. Listen carefully to virtuosos' performances and try to realize how they achieve their exquisite niceties.

However hard you may practice every day, it would be impossible to become skilful in a month or so. This passage will provide a great deal of study material.

楽譜どおりに弾くことはそれほどむずかしいことではない。しかしこれを美しく立派に弾く人は極めて少ない。名手達の演奏に注意し、いかに妙味を発揮して弾いているかに気づかなければならない。たとえ毎日練習しても短期間の訓練で立派になり得るわけがありません。この所は最も学習のために役にたつよい小節であると思う。

Fundamental Exercise　基本練習

The bowing indication at lusingando (p) is what Joachim designated. Try it.

We should always appreciate and carefully study what has been recommended by Joachim, a great musician of profound and varied attainments.

lusingando（*p*）のところの楽譜の下に示した弓はヨアヒムの示した弓です。試みてください。

極めて博学であり深い研究をなしたヨアヒムの示すところのものを深く味わい研究すべきです。

Point of Practice　　学習の仕方

Fundamental Exercise　基本練習

G線上の音階
Scale on the G string

Point of Practice　　学習の仕方

Pitches are likely to become inaccurate at the shift, for example, from the third position to the second. Strict training is required to obtain exact pitches.

サード・ポジションからセカンド・ポジションへの移動 など，音程が不正確になり易いところですから，訓練に よって正確さを獲得すべきです。

Fundamental Exercise　基本練習

2と1の指をつける。
Keep the second and first fingers close together.

Point of Practice　　学習の仕方

Fundamental Exercise　基本練習

Point of Practice

学習の仕方

Pierre Rode's Chromatic Fingering

Pierre Rode, noted for his violin concertos, was born in 1744 at Bordeaux, France and died in 1830 near Damazan. He was a pupil of Viotti and was a professor at the Paris Conservatoire. The excellent chromatic fingering he developed has now come to be accepted by many people.

ピエール・ロード（Pierre Rode）の Chromatic Fingering について。
バイオリン協奏曲でピエール・ロードの名前はよく人に知られている。彼は Viotti の弟子で1774年フランスのボルドーで生まれ、パリ音楽院の教授になり、1830年ダマゾンで没した大家である。彼の考案したすぐれた半音階の指使いは、現在多くの人々に用いられるようになってきた。

Basically it is made up as follows:

    (Ascending) 1 2 3   2 3 4 0
    (Descending) 0 4 3 2   3 2 1 0

上行   1 2 3 2 3 4 0
下行   0 4 3 2 3 2 1 0   }を基本としたものである。

正確な音程へ熟練すること。

Practise until you can be sure of obtaining correct pitches.

The chromatic fingering is characterized by the clarity of each tone, which is produced without letting fingers slide, and which is as clear as if the chromatic scale were played on the piano keyboard.

半音階指使いの特長は、指をずらせることなく各音鮮明に、ちょうどピアノの鍵盤上で半音階を弾くように鮮かであること。

Point of Practice　　　学習の仕方

The change of strings is so difficult here that many pupils become desperate or confused. To gain sufficient skill. It is particularly necessary to learn how to count correctly and to attain enough technique for changing strings.

Do the exercise every day carefully and repeatedly, and try to avoid unevenness.

これは移弦のむずかしいところで、多くの生徒はここであせったり混乱したりする。易しそうでけっして易しくなく、十分熟練を要するところです。とくに拍子のとり方、移弦のうまさを習熟する必要がある。

毎日ていねいに繰り返し練習し、乱れをなくすように。

Point of Practice　　　学習の仕方

As usual in the old notation, the first note of this figure, which is not a note of the chord, is written like this:

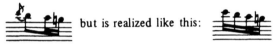

古典の書法として、このはじめの音は和声外の音から始まる場合に記され、と演奏されます。

Since Mozart himself did not clearly differentiate this point in his notation, later performers seem to have interpreted this notation according to their idea of how it might have been executed in Mozart's days. Joachim, too, indicated two alternatives;

モーツァルト自身がこの点をあまり刻明に区別して記していなかったために、後から演奏者たちが、実際に演奏されたであろうものを想像して、いろいろ区分して弾いているのではないかと考えられます。

ヨアヒムもこの点について2つを示している。

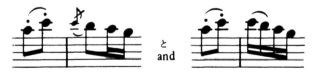

The notation chosen here is what has been widely adopted among performers.

ここには、今日多くの演奏家が弾いている方法を採り上げた。

44

Point of Practice　学習の仕方

ここで左手の形をととのえ、2と3の指を迅速に動かすトリルの準備練習をする。

Fix the posture of the left hand, and move the second and the third fingers rapidly in preparation for playing the trill.

はじめはゆっくり弾く。
Play slowly at first.

Point of Practice　学習の仕方

Point of Practice　　学習の仕方

音程を正確にする訓練。
Play intervals accurately.

Do not proceed to practising the cadenza before you have enough drill in these figures.
First practise without playing the trills, then add them when you have gained sufficient skill.

これらを十分訓練した後にカデンツの練習に入ってください。最初はトリルなしで練習し，熟練したうえでトリルを加える。

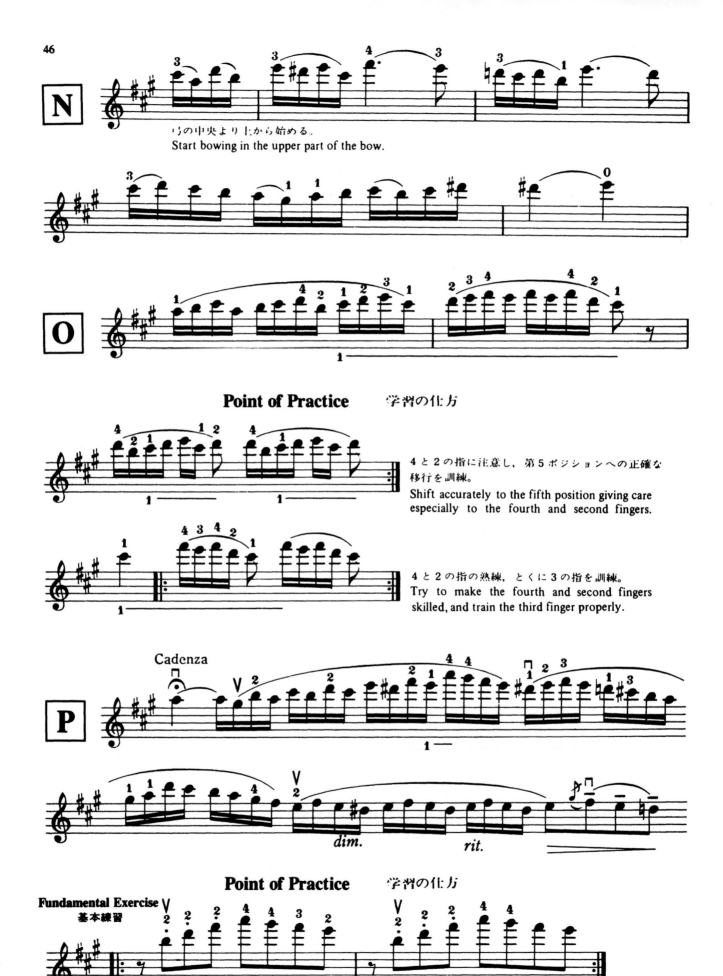

46

N

りの中央より上から始める。
Start bowing in the upper part of the bow.

O

Point of Practice 学習の仕方

4と2の指に注意し，第5ポジションへの正確な移行を訓練。
Shift accurately to the fifth position giving care especially to the fourth and second fingers.

4と2の指の熟練，とくに3の指を訓練。
Try to make the fourth and second fingers skilled, and train the third finger properly.

Cadenza

P

dim.

rit.

Point of Practice 学習の仕方

Fundamental Exercise
基本練習

Concentrate on gaining accurate pitches.　正確な音程を得る練習。

Counting accurately, practise this figure until you
can repeat it fluently.

Train the first and third fingers for correct pitches,
and each finger for accurate shift.

1と3の指の音程と指の移動の練習。

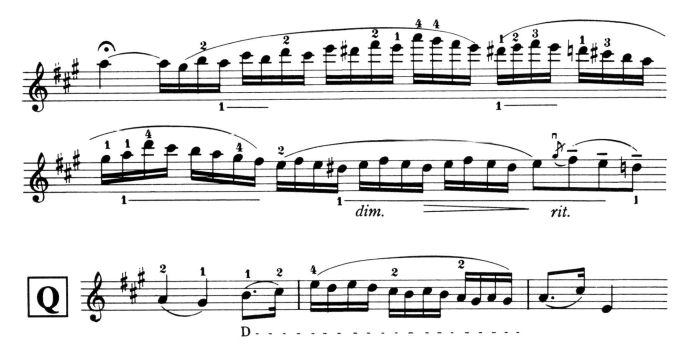

Point of Practice　　学習の仕方

In playing [figure], pitches often become inaccurate and the rhythm easily becomes uneven. Since the
reason is insufficient practice on the D string, pupils
need to do these exercises repeatedly every day.

音程が不正確になりやすく拍子がそろいにくい。D弦で
彈くためであり、D弦上の練習不足のためであるので毎
日繰り返す必要がある。